10.12.18
$24.95
AS-14

10/18

Withdrawn

D0949967

CHARACTERS

CHARACTERS
An Ancient Take on Bad Behavior

THEOPHRASTUS

Introduction and Annotations
JAMES ROMM

Translation
PAMELA MENSCH

Illustrations
ANDRÉ CARRILHO

Graphic Design
DON QUAINTANCE

CALLAWAY

NEW YORK
2018

Oh Times! Oh Manners! It is my opinion
That you are changing sadly your dominion—
I mean the reign of manners hath long ceased,
For men have none at all, or bad at least.

—Edgar Allan Poe
Oh, Tempora! Oh, Mores!, ca. 1825

Contents

Theophrastus and His *Characters*

JAMES ROMM

I N THE BEGINNING OF TIME, when the Greek goddess Night gave birth to Sleep, and Death, and Dreams, she also bore the curious figure of Momus, the god of faultfinding. So at least claims Hesiod's *Theogony*, a text of the eighth century BC, the starting point of Momus's long, majestic reign.

Though he lacked the thunderbolt of Zeus and the aegis of Athena, Momus had the gift of a special kind of vision: he could see flaws and shortcomings everywhere, even in the gods among whom he dwelt. When contemplating Aphrodite, the embodiment of radiant beauty, he noted that one of her sandals squeaked. Such clarity of sight made Momus a threat to the other deities, who banished him from their company and exiled him to the world of men—where he has remained ever since.

Before his departure from Olympus, Momus was asked to judge the handiwork of his fellow gods, each of whom strove to create something that could escape all censure. Poseidon proudly produced a stately and powerful bull; Momus sized up the gorgeous animal and observed that its eyes had been poorly placed, for whenever the bull lowered its head and leveled its horns for a charge, it could no longer see where it was going. This little Aesopic fable was well known among Athenians of the late fourth century BC, for Aristotle, in his biological treatise *On the Parts of Animals*, pauses to take note of it.

The spirit of Momus indeed walked abroad in the Athens of that day. Diogenes, the Cynic philosopher, prowled the streets searching for an honest man, holding up his storied lantern. His student, Crates of Thebes, another Cynic who had made his home in the city, coined a maxim that might have come from Momus himself: "It's impossible to find a person without flaws; just like in a pomegranate, there's always some rotten seed."

Terracotta sculptors at this time began producing new kinds of figurines: hyperrealistic portrayals of the elderly, the obese, the misshapen. Displayed in modern museums and commonly called "grotesques," these statuettes are sometimes identified as actors in comic dramas, but that's often a curator's guess, based on their effect on the viewer. These deformed creatures, with their exaggerated failings, their departures from the idealized forms seen in earlier Greek art, invite us to laugh. Comedy, Aristotle wrote in the *Poetics*, is about people we regard as worse than ourselves.

Also at this time, an author named Theophrastus, a favorite student and close friend of Aristotle, set aside his studies of philosophy and natural science to compose the work known as *Characters*. Holding high the lantern of Diogenes, he cut open the human pomegranate to find its rotten seeds, creating, around 320 BC, thirty vivid studies of the foibles of his contemporaries, each personality type sketched with startling acuity. He worked from no template. No one before him had ever composed such verbal portraits, though many have done so since: Joseph Hall in the sixteenth century, Jean de la Bruyère in the seventeenth, and George Eliot in the nineteenth, to name but a few.

Theophrastus's thirty paragons of bad behavior now parade before us again, clad in the finery of a new translation and contemporary depictions. A festival of faultfinding unfolds on every page, proving the enduring potency of Momus's reign on earth. Long live the king!

THEOPHRASTUS CAME TO ATHENS some two or three decades before writing *Characters*, a transplant from the island of Lesbos. He was called Tyrtamus then, and his name and manner of speech—both colored by his native Aeolic dialect—marked him as an outsider. Aristotle, whose favorite student he soon became, rechristened him with a more Attic-sounding nickname, Theophrastus, meaning "Divine in speech." In classical Athens, however, a foreigner might be renamed but not naturalized, as Aristotle, himself an immigrant from Stagira in the Chalcidice, had already learned.

In legal terms, Theophrastus and Aristotle were "metics," resident aliens, who had no political rights and could not own property. Native-born Athenians, even women who also lacked political rights, might look down on such men. Cicero tells how Theophrastus once asked an old woman in the market about the price for her goods; in a scornful reply, she addressed him as *hospes* (presumably Cicero's Latin translation of Greek *xenos*), or "foreigner." Spoken by someone of low social rank, that epithet was meant to put Theophrastus in his place. Though he might acquire fine Attic speech and join Aristotle's high-minded school, he was still a "bowl carrier"—the derogatory term was glossed by Theophrastus himself, in a work now lost, as a reference to metics in Athenian state processions who were set apart by the bowls they were made to carry.

Theophrastus was an outsider to Athens in other terms as well. He made his home in the Lyceum, a space beyond the ancient city's walls (though well within the bounds of modern Athens, assuming that the 1996 finds near Rigillis Street are indeed the Lyceum's remains). Originally a public grove with a gymnasium and a *peripatos*, or covered walkway, the Lyceum had gradually been taken over, in the last third of the fourth century BC, by Aristotle and his students, who later became known as the Peripatetics, "those of the walkway." This fraternal place was not just a theater for lectures but a setting for meals, social gatherings, and research—the first college campus, or perhaps the second, since Plato's Academy had been established earlier along similar lines. But the Lyceum, unlike the Academy, was attended mostly by non-Athenians.

To judge by his will, preserved by Diogenes Laertius (a late Greek biographer), Theophrastus cared deeply for the *philia*, the spirit of friendship and community, that was fostered at the Lyceum. That document tells us nearly all we know about the physical setting of the Lyceum and Theophrastus's life there. By the time he wrote it, Theophrastus had come to own property on the Lyceum grounds—a privilege arranged for him by friends in high places—and he bequeathed this to a group of ten "sharers," men who "wish to practice philosophy and learn together there," further stipulating that "all hold it in common, like a sanctuary, living, as is fitting and just, on familiar and friendly terms with one another."

Theophrastus could afford such largesse, for his will demonstrates that he was rich, the owner of large properties and at least nine slaves, perhaps many more. His wealth and generosity stand in sharp contrast to what is found in *Characters*, where he shows a Dickensian fascination with meanness in matters of money. No fewer than three of his thirty sketches—the Miser, Chiseler, and Pinchpenny— are defined by that trait, and many others exhibit it here and there. None of these tightwads, it should be noted, are poor men; the Chiseler is well enough off to employ a household staff, though he shorts their grain rations by banging upward the bottom of his metal measuring cup. Theophrastus, for his part, left a bequest of 2000 drachmas—several years' worth of income for an average wage earner—to a slave named Pompylus, who went on to become a philosopher himself.

Theophrastus likely had no wife or children, since none are mentioned in his will. Perhaps, as is often assumed of Plato and his academicians, the male fellowship of the philosophic school either substituted for, or included, bonds of sexual intimacy. Rumor assigned him infatuations with both Aristotle's daughter, Pythias, and son, Nicomachus. Among the list of his essays recorded by Diogenes Laertius, one finds two separate treatises titled "On Love," revealing a certain interest in the subject, though not much of one—these are only two essays out of more than two hundred (almost all have perished).

To judge by Diogenes' list, Theophrastus wrote on a wide array of topics, ranging from the sublime ("On the Gods," "On Celestial Bodies") to the ridiculous ("On Sweating," "On Honey," "On Hair"). Botany does not seem to have been a particular interest, though he is today considered the father of that field due to the chance preservation of most of his "Inquiry into Plants" and "Causes of Plants." Other odd bits of his natural histories—studies of stones, and of the signs that foretell coming weather—have also survived. Strangely, nothing in these treatises bears any resemblance to *Characters* or shares any of its humor. A few scholars have therefore doubted the attribution to Theophrastus of this work, but most have accepted the idea that a sober man of science can, perhaps in private moments or in pages seen only by friends, indulge a taste for satire, caricature, and lampoon.

Theophrastus lived through an age that saw Macedon, the monarchic province in the north of Greece, rise to global hegemony under the rule of Philip and Alexander the Great. His adopted home, Athens, was politically divided, the upper class tending to align with the new Macedonian order while the masses agitated for defiance and, after Alexander's death in 323 BC, revolt. His mentor Aristotle, being Alexander's former tutor, left Athens under a cloud of suspicion when that revolt broke out; he died of an illness shortly thereafter. Theophrastus was also linked to the Macedonians but, interestingly, did not fall into similar disfavor. Even when Hagnonides, a radical democrat and staunch Macedon-hater, got him indicted on a politically motivated charge, Theophrastus, according to the report of Diogenes Laertius, embarrassed him by winning nearly four-fifths of the jurors' votes.

New complexities arose for Theophrastus when the Macedonians installed one of his students, Demetrius of Phalerum, as puppet leader of an oligarchic government in 317 BC. When democracy was restored a decade later and

Demetrius thrown out, Theophrastus was vulnerable to reprisals. On the motion of a certain Sophocles (not the famous playwright), he was exiled from Athens along with the heads of the other philosophic schools. But a new motion only a year later invited them all back and allowed Theophrastus to resume his leadership of the Lyceum. The city had no appetite "to sin twice against philosophy" (the words are Aristotle's), having long regretted its execution of Socrates, almost a century earlier, following a similar change of regime.

Such political tergiversations, which must have caused the average Athenian grave concern, are nearly invisible in *Characters*. The people depicted there go about their routines, undisturbed by, or even unaware of, the events swirling around them. An exception is the Newshound, who likes to report on the twists and turns in the Wars of the Successors—the chaotic power struggle among Alexander the Great's generals that began after Alexander's death. But even the Newshound seems uninformed, since the story he spreads about a recent battle is false and perhaps invented. The Authoritarian (or an "Oligarchic Man," an antidemocrat) might be expected to make reference to the Macedonians, his natural allies, but doesn't, and his exhortation to "get free of the mob and the marketplace," the centers of democratic ferment, could have been spoken by an Athenian conservative of any era.

The last two decades of Theophrastus's life, following his return to Athens in 306 BC, seem to have been an untroubled stretch of popularity and productivity. Diogenes Laertius reports that two thousand Athenians used to attend his philosophic discourses, presumably in the afternoons when members of the Lyceum lectured to the general public (morning lessons were for the inner circle). The size of the crowd must have pleased him, but its composition didn't; in a letter to a fellow Peripatetic (a passage preserved by Diogenes), he complained that "to get an audience...of the sort one desires is not easy." To command attention from his auditors, he reportedly used parodic gestures, such as licking his lips with exaggerated delight to play the gourmet— a pantomime version, perhaps, of his technique in *Characters*.

Theophrastus died unremarkably, at age 85, and, according to Diogenes, his body was carried to the grave by a procession of "all the Athenians." That means the Busybody was there to say farewell, as were the Yokel, the Dullard, the Charlatan, and the Coward. Perhaps the Shameless Man disrupted the funeral by exposing himself to passing women, the Obnoxious Man by belching loudly, and the Babbler by his noisy and inane comments to his neighbors. Then, when the ceremony was over, all went back to wheedling, flattering, and deceiving one another, profiteering from loans, giving offense with poor hygiene and inappropriate speech, and otherwise indulging the bad habits and bizarre quirks of behavior that made them who they were, and who they remain today.

WHEN THE PERSIAN KING CYRUS THE GREAT first encountered a delegation of Spartan ambassadors, he asked some Greeks in his retinue who the Spartans were. His advisors described the life of a typical Greek city, whereupon Cyrus turned contemptuous. "I have never yet feared the sort of men who have set a place in the middle of their city where they come together and cheat each other under oath," he scoffed. He meant the agora, a characteristically Greek, though not particularly Spartan, institution—a place not just for buying and selling (regarded by Cyrus as a form of cheating) but for seeing and being seen, showing off wealth or status, and generally defining one's social role. This central urban space of Athenian society is thus central to *Characters* as well.

The mercantilism of Theophrastus's Athens, its overriding concern with getting and spending, is part of what makes *Characters* such a resonant work in the era of late-stage capitalism. No matter what his defining trait, money and consumer goods are much on the mind of *homo Theophrasticus*. The Talker prattles on about how cheaply wheat can be purchased; the Yokel asks passersby about the prices of goatskins and salted fish; the Flatterer praises his host's dinnerware; and virtually everyone buys, sells, lends, borrows, collects on debts, assesses interest, totals up sums, "pockets" coins by placing them in their cheeks, and generally takes part in the vast, unregulated economic network that pervaded classical Athens.

Apart from this one work, and the comedies of Aristophanes that preceded it, classical authors rarely give insight into this economic life. The Greek poets set their epics and dramas in a pre-monetary mythic world; Plato, in his *Republic*, described an ideal state in which private property would be forbidden to the elite. Theophrastus, however, his senses perhaps sharpened by his botanical research, delighted in the physicality and corporeality of his Athenian subjects. He observes their food, their clothes, their purchases, the décor of their homes. He notices objects we never hear of elsewhere, like the spurs worn by the Social Climber to show he's wealthy enough to ride in the cavalry, or— unforgettable in its specificity—the little shield and ladder that same man buys for his pet bird, so it can impress visitors by acting out the part of a hoplite soldier besieging an enemy city.

As a wealthy man who didn't need to work, and who lived in the rarefied enclosure of the Lyceum, Theophrastus might have found the concerns of the agora contemptible, yet the tone of *Characters* is surprisingly not condescending. The Authoritarian, who advises his friends to "get free of the mob and the marketplace," is lampooned here, as well as the Arrogant Man, who won't deign to join his own dinner guests or let anyone see him eat. Such men were closer to Theophrastus in social rank than the Slovenly Man, Yokel, and Obnoxious Man, yet all are exposed to the glare of his arc lights. The great humanity of *Characters* lies in this: no one is spared. All share alike in the petty vices that define the human condition.

Characters is itself an agora, a market square of misbehaviors, which the reader is allowed to observe from a comfortable *al fresco* table. Like Puccini's Schaunard, the cynic who drinks at the aptly named Café Momus in *La Bohème*, we may declare, as we observe the panorama of peccadilloes, "*la commedia è stupenda!*" Enjoyment comes guilt-free, because nothing we see causes grave harm. The court appearances often referred to in *Characters* stem merely from civil lawsuits, not criminal trials. There are no lessons learned; no moral scheme demands punishment for wrongs. Only the Senseless Man goes to jail, and apparently only for failure to pay his debts.

Early editors of *Characters* did not approve of this blithely nonpunitive spirit. In an effort to make the text *teach* something, they added quasi-Aristotelian definitions as a heading to each sketch, and, in some cases, moralizing or reproachful conclusions at their ends. These interpolated elements are easily spotted and have been excised by modern editors, as they have been omitted here.

Other alterations to the text, however, are not so easily repaired. Gaps and holes arising from its long process of transmission, more numerous than in most ancient works, have rendered some passages unintelligible; these we have for the most part skipped. In a few cases, where a textual corruption does not completely obliterate sense, we have included the damaged sentence but indicated an unfilled gap, with an ellipsis enclosed by brackets: [...]. In this we follow the Greek text edited by James Diggle (Cambridge University Press, 2004), the text on which Pamela Mensch has based her translation.

All our editorial and design choices in this volume, in particular André Carrilho's illustrations, are intended to bring out the text's comic energy and irrepressible vitality. Few literary works preserved from antiquity offer us so much pleasure, while requiring so little in the way of background knowledge or interpretive skill. Few evoke so vividly the daily realities of ancient Athens: the bustle of its squares, the jostling in its streets, the gossip in its porticoes, the banter in its private homes.

So take your seat at the Café Momus and prepare to enjoy Theophrastus's pageant of human imperfections. *La commedia è stupenda!*

CHARACTERS

CHARACTERS

If he's heard or seen something, he pretends he hasn't.

THE DISSEMBLER

THE **D**ISSEMBLER[1] IS THE SORT who goes up to his enemies to chat with them. He praises in their presence men he's attacked behind their backs and consoles them when they've lost in court.[2] He pardons those who malign him and smiles at their reproaches. He tells people eager to meet with him to come back later and won't ever admit what he's up to, but says he's thinking things over, pretends that he's just returned home, and says that it's late and that he's under the weather. If he's heard or seen something, he pretends he hasn't. If he's agreed to something, he says he doesn't recall it. In some instances he says that he'll look into it, in others that he doesn't know, in others that he's surprised, and in still others that *he* used to think that way himself. And in general he's apt to use expressions like "I don't believe it," "I can't imagine so," "I'm astonished," "But that's not what he told *me*," "It seems incredible," "Tell it to someone else," "I'm at a loss whether to believe *you* or disbelieve *him*," and "Don't be too trusting."

He says that the man's foot is better proportioned than the shoe.

THE FLATTERER

THE *FLATTERER IS THE SORT* who, when walking with someone,[3] says, "Do you notice how people are gazing at you? You're the only one in the city who attracts so much attention," and "You were praised yesterday in the stoa."[4] (When more than thirty men, sitting there idly, found themselves discussing who was their best man, everyone, beginning with the flatterer, came round to naming the flatterer's favorite.) While saying such things, he removes some lint from the man's cloak,[5] and if some wind-blown straw lands in the man's hair, he plucks it out; laughing, he says, "You see? Since I haven't been with you for two days, your beard is full of gray hairs, though *you*, even at your age, have dark hair." While the man is speaking, the flatterer urges everyone else to be quiet and praises him when he's within earshot. He signals his approval when the man pauses, saying, "Quite right," and if the man makes a joke that falls flat, he laughs aloud and thrusts his cloak into his mouth as if he can't contain his laughter. He urges people approaching them to wait until his favorite has passed by. He buys apples and pears for the man's children, offers these while the man is watching, and when kissing the youngsters, says, "Nestlings of a worthy father." When shopping with him for boots, he says that the man's foot is better proportioned than the shoe. If the man is

on his way to visit a friend, the flatterer runs ahead and says, "He's on his way to you," and, on turning around, says, "I've announced you." At a dinner he's the first guest to praise the wine, and he remarks to his host (by whom he's sitting), "What an elegant spread!" Lifting one of the dishes from the table, he says, "How good this is!" He asks the man if he's cold and wants a cloak, and in the course of speaking wraps a blanket around him. He stoops to whisper in the man's ear and is always glancing toward him while chatting with others. At the theater he gets the cushions from the slave and takes it upon himself to spread them out for his friend. He declares that the man's house is well designed, his farm well cultivated, and his portrait an exact likeness.

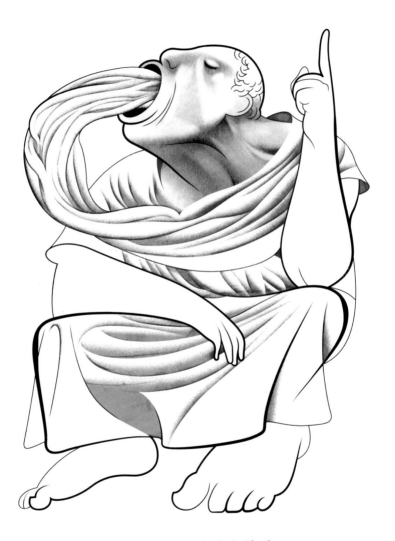

He then relates in detail what he had for dinner.

THE TALKER

THE ALKER IS THE SORT who plumps himself down next to someone he doesn't know and starts praising his own wife; he goes on to describe the dream he had the night before and then relates in detail what he had for dinner. As the conversation proceeds, he remarks that people are much worse nowadays than they were in the past, and that wheat is going cheap in the marketplace, and that there are lots of foreigners in town, and that the sea has been fit for sailing since the Dionysia,[6] and that if there's more rain, the soil will improve; and which field he's going to cultivate next year; and that it's hard to make a living; and that Damippus raised an enormous torch at the Mysteries.[7] "How many pillars are there in the Odeon?" "I threw up yesterday!" "What day is it today?" "The Mysteries are held in the month of Boedromion, the Apaturia in Pyanepsion, and the country Dionysia in Poseideon."[8] And if you stand for this, he'll never stop.

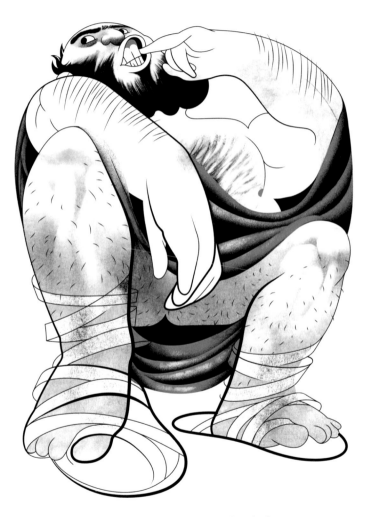

When seated he draws his cloak above his knee.

THE YOKEL

THE YOKEL IS THE SORT who downs some curds and whey before entering the Assembly[9] and declares that perfume smells no sweeter than garlic. He wears sandals too large for his feet. He talks in a loud voice. He distrusts his friends and relatives; he'd rather discuss his most important affairs with his slaves. He gives his hired laborers on the farm all the news from the Assembly. When seated he draws his cloak above his knee.[10] He's never charmed or captivated by anything in the street, but whenever he catches sight of an ox, an ass, or a goat, he'll stand there gazing at it. He's apt to eat food as he's taking it from the storeroom; he takes his wine straight up.[11] He makes stealthy passes at his baker-woman and grinds the corn with her whenever he's measuring out provisions for himself and his whole household. While taking his own breakfast, he feeds his yoke-animals. He answers the door himself,[12] and when he's called his dog and grabbed him by the snout, he says, "This one guards our hearth and home." He rejects a silver coin he's received from someone, since it looks too much like lead, and tries to exchange it for another. If he's lent someone a plow, basket, sickle, or sack, he asks for it back in the middle of the night, having remembered it while lying awake. He sings at the baths and hammers nails into his shoes.[13] On his way to town he asks anyone he meets how much goatskin hides and salted fish are going for,[14] and whether it's the first of the month,[15] and says that the moment he gets to town, he wants to have his hair cut and fetch some salted fish from Archias' since he's heading that way.

The sort who conveys his admiration in the warmest terms.

THE SYCOPHANT

THE SYCOPHANT IS DOUBTLESS the sort who hails you from a distance, addresses you as "my good man," conveys his admiration in the warmest terms, takes hold of you with both hands, walks on with you a little way, asks when he'll see you again, and offers his compliments as he departs. When summoned to an arbitration, he wants to gratify not only the party he sides with, but the man's opponent as well, so that he'll be thought impartial. He tells foreigners that their arguments are sounder than those of his fellow citizens. When invited to dinner, he asks his host to summon the children. When they arrive, he says they resemble their father more than peas in a pod. He draws them close and kisses them and seats them beside him, joining some of them in their game, calling out "wineskin!" and "axe!"[16] while letting the others fall asleep on his lap, though they're crushing him.

The sort who dances the cordax while sober.

THE SENSELESS MAN

SENSELESS MAN IS THE SORT who dances the cordax while sober.[17] At street fairs he goes around collecting small change from everyone in attendance and fighting with those who already have tickets or insist they can see what they like without paying. He's apt to be an inn- or a brothel-keeper or a tax-gatherer, and to reject no job as beneath him: he'll work as an auctioneer, a cook, or a gambler. He lets his mother go hungry, gets hauled in for theft, and spends more time in prison than at home. In court he's capable of being at one time a defendant and at another a plaintiff, and at yet another of taking an oath in order to get a case dismissed, and of arriving in court with a potful of evidence in the folds of his cloak and batches of little notes in his hands. He doesn't scruple to take charge of a bunch of peddlers, lending them money readily, charging them interest at the rate of three half-obols per drachma per day,[18] and making the rounds of the cookshops and the stalls where fresh and salted fish are sold, storing in his cheeks the interest he's accumulated from his dealings.[19]

The other man can't get a word in edgewise.

THE BABBLER

THE **B**ABBLER IS THE SORT who says to anyone he meets, regardless of what that man says to him, that he's talking nonsense and that he himself understands the whole thing and that the man will learn something about it if he listens to him. Midway through the man's reply, he throws in, "Now don't forget what you were going to say," "Good of you to remind me," "It's helpful to chat," "I failed to mention that," "You're quick to catch my drift," and "I've been waiting to see whether you'd come around to my point of view." He throws in other such side comments, and as a result the other man can't get a word in edgewise. Once he's exhausted individuals, he's apt to go up to whole groups of people and put them to flight though they're in the midst of conducting business. Venturing into the schools and wrestling grounds, he disrupts the students' lessons. When people say they have to leave, he's apt to accompany them and see them home. To those who inquire, he reports what's happening in the Assembly and throws in an account of the battle fought at the time of Aristophon the orator, as well as the one among the Lacedemonians in Lysander's day,[20] and describes the speeches he himself once gave that won him renown in the Assembly. And when, in the

41

course of relating these matters, he gets around to denouncing the masses,[21] his hearers either interrupt, nod off, or walk away while he's still talking. On a jury he prevents his fellow jurors from reaching a verdict, in the theater his fellow spectators from watching the play, and at a dinner, his fellow guests from consuming their food. He says, "It's hard for me to be silent," and that his tongue is supple and that he would not keep quiet even if he appeared more talkative than the swallows. He puts up with being teased by his own children: whenever he wants to go to bed, they prevent him by saying, "Prattle to us a little, daddy, so we can get to sleep."

"Then I guess I'll have to feast you with the latest."

THE NEWSHOUND

THE NEWSHOUND IS THE SORT who, the moment he meets his friend, asks with a smile, "Where have you been?" and "What do you have to report?" and "How are you?" But before the man can say, "I'm well," he interrupts with, "You ask if there's any news? Indeed, there are some good things to report." Giving his friend no time to reply, he says, "What do you mean? Have you really heard *nothing*? Then I guess I'll have to feast you with the latest." He's got someone who's just returned from the battle itself—either a soldier or a slave of Asteius the flute player or Lycon the contractor—from whom he says he heard the story. He relates that Polyperchon and the king have prevailed in battle and that Cassander has been taken prisoner.[22] If someone asks him, "Do you believe it?" he'll say he does, since it's the talk of the town, and the story is gaining ground, and everyone is of the same opinion. He says that the bloodshed was immense. He says he's read the signs in the faces of their public men; he's noticed that all are changed. He says he's also overheard that they've got someone hidden in a private house—a man who arrived four days earlier from Macedonia and knows the whole story. Relating all these matters, he somehow imagines he sounds sincere when he cries, "Unfortunate Cassander! Unhappy wretch! Do you see how fickle fortune can be?" and "Be sure to keep this to yourself."

If he gets away with it, fine and dandy.

THE SHAMELESS MAN

THE SHAMELESS MAN IS THE SORT who, after short-changing someone, goes back to ask him for a loan. After sacrificing to the gods, he salts the meat, stores it away, and goes to someone else's house for dinner. He even invites his slave along, offers him meat and bread from the table, and in everyone's hearing says, "Enjoy your supper, Tibeius!" When shopping he reminds the butcher of any favors he has done him. And then, standing next to the scale, he throws on some meat, preferably, or otherwise a bone, for his soup. If he gets away with it, fine and dandy. If not, he grabs some ox guts from the table and goes away laughing. When his foreign guests have bought theater tickets, he joins them without paying for his seat, and does the same the next day, on which occasion he includes his sons and their tutor in the party. Whenever someone's bought something cheap, he asks that he himself be given a share. He goes to another's house to borrow barley or bran and obliges the lenders of these goods to have them delivered to him. He's apt, at the baths, to go up to the bronze tanks, dip in his ladle (despite the bath-man's shouting), and douse himself, saying on his way out that he's already bathed […] "no thanks to you!"

He won't let anyone pick up an olive or date that's fallen to the ground.

THE MISER

THE MISER IS THE SORT who demands the repayment of a half-obol by the end of the month.[23] At a communal supper, he keeps count of how many glasses each man has drunk, and the initial libation he pours to Artemis is smaller than that of any of his fellow diners. When a servant breaks a clay pot or plate, he deducts the cost from the man's rations. If his wife drops a three-penny piece, he's likely to move the furniture, couches, and chests, and to rummage through the trash. If he sells something, he charges so much that the buyer always gets the worst of the bargain. He won't let anyone eat figs from his garden, or walk through his field, or pick up an olive or date that's fallen to the ground. He checks his boundaries every day to make sure they remain unchanged.[24] He's apt to exact a fee for late payment and to charge compound interest. When giving a dinner for his fellow townsmen he serves them tiny portions of meat. When he goes food shopping he returns without having bought anything. He forbids his wife to lend anyone salt or a lampwick or cumin or marjoram or barley groats or wreaths or barley cakes,[25] maintaining that over the course of a year these many small things add up to a lot.

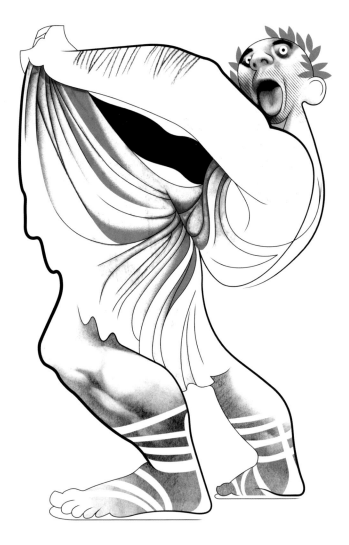

The sort who pulls up his clothes and flashes his genitals.

THE OBNOXIOUS MAN

OBNOXIOUS MAN IS THE SORT who, when he encounters freeborn women, pulls up his clothes and flashes his genitals. In the theater he applauds when everyone else has stopped, and hisses actors whom the rest of the audience take pleasure in watching; and when the audience is silent, he throws back his head and belches to make the spectators turn around. When the marketplace is crowded he visits the shops that sell nuts, myrtle berries, and fruits, and munches on these items while chatting with the seller. He hails by name a bystander with whom he's not acquainted. When he sees people in a hurry to get somewhere, he urges them to wait. He goes up to a man who's leaving the law court after losing an important case and congratulates him. He buys himself some food, hires flute girls, shows these purchases to anyone he meets, and offers to share them.[26] Stopping at a barbershop or a perfume stand, he says he's planning to get drunk.

The sort who comes to solicit advice from someone who's busy.

THE TACTLESS MAN

THE TACTLESS MAN IS THE SORT who comes to solicit advice from someone who's busy. He serenades his sweetheart when she's down with a fever. He approaches a man who's just had to forfeit bail money and asks him to post bail for him. He turns up to give evidence in a case that's already been adjudicated. At a wedding where he's a guest, he delivers a diatribe against women. He invites someone who's just arrived after a long journey to go for a walk. He's apt to bring to someone who's just concluded a sale a buyer willing to pay more. For the benefit of those who have listened and understood he gets up to explain things all over again. He eagerly puts himself out to get you what you don't want but can't bring yourself to refuse. He shows up to collect an interest payment from people engaged in performing a costly sacrifice. Standing next to a house slave being whipped, he remarks that a slave of *his* who once received a beating of that sort later hanged himself. Present at an arbitration, he sets the disputants at odds, though both are ready to be reconciled. Eager to dance, he takes hold of a fellow who's not yet drunk.

When the doctor forbids it, she generously plies the patient with drink.

THE BUSYBODY

THE **B**USYBODY IS THE SORT who stands up and promises what he can't deliver. In court when it's agreed that his argument is just, he overdoes it and loses his case. He makes his slave mix more wine than his company can possibly drink. He tries to separate the parties in a fight even if he doesn't know them. When he's leading others along a shortcut, he can't find the way to his destination. He goes up to the general and asks him when he's going to deploy his troops and what orders he'll give the day after tomorrow. He goes to his father and says that his mother is already asleep in their bedroom. When the doctor forbids him to give wine to an invalid, he says he wants to perform an experiment and generously plies the patient with drink. When a woman has died, he inscribes on her tomb the names of her husband, father, and mother, that of the woman herself, and her place of birth, and adds, "All of these were good and worthy persons."[27] When he's about to swear an oath, he says to the bystanders, "I've had plenty of experience swearing oaths."

Scheduled to appear in court, he forgets all about it and goes to the country.

THE DULLARD

THE **D**ULLARD IS THE SORT who, when he's reckoned a sum with an abacus and arrived at a total, asks the person sitting next to him, "What does it come to?" When he's the defendant in a lawsuit and is scheduled to appear in court, he forgets all about it and goes to the country. Attending a play, he falls asleep in the theater and is left behind alone. Having overeaten at dinner, he visits the outhouse at night and is bitten by the neighbor's dog. When he's acquired something and put it away himself, he later searches high and low but can't find it. When the death of a friend is reported to him so that he can attend the funeral, he looks downcast, sheds a tear, and says, "Thank goodness!" He's apt, when receiving money owed to him, to bring along witnesses. Though it's wintertime, he scolds his slave for not buying cucumbers. Making his sons wrestle and run races with him, he drives them to exhaustion. On the farm, boiling himself some lentil soup, he salts the pot twice, making the soup inedible. When it's raining, he says, "How sweet the stars smell," though everyone else says "the earth." When someone says, "How many corpses do you imagine have been carried out for burial at the Erian Gates?" he replies, "You and I should only have so many!"

The sort who says, "Don't bother me."

THE SURLY MAN

THE **S**URLY MAN IS THE SORT who, when asked, "Where is someone-or-other?" says, "Don't bother me." When addressed he doesn't respond. When offering something for sale, he won't tell prospective buyers how much he's selling it for, but asks, "What will it fetch?" He can't forgive a person who dirties him by accident or shoves him or steps on his foot. To a friend who asks him to contribute to a loan he says he won't give anything, but arrives later with the cash and says he's throwing his money away. If he trips on the street he's apt to curse the stone. He won't wait long for anyone. He'll refuse to sing or make a speech or dance. He won't even offer thanks to the gods.

He bathes vigorously, summons priestesses, and tells them to purify him thoroughly.

The Superstitious Man

THE **S**UPERSTITIOUS MAN IS THE SORT who, after washing his hands in a spring, sprinkling himself with holy water from a shrine, and sticking a sprig of laurel in his mouth, embarks on his daily rounds.[28] If a weasel runs across his path, he will not take a step until someone else has walked past the spot or he's thrown three stones over the road. Suppose he sees a snake in the house: if it's reddish-brown, he invokes Sabazius; if it's a holy one, he erects a hero shrine right then and there.[29] Whenever he walks past the shiny stones at the crossroads he anoints them with olive oil from his flask,[30] falls to his knees, and prostrates himself before he departs. If a mouse nibbles through a sack of barley, he goes to his spiritual director to ask what he should do. And if the man replies that he should give the sack to the tanner to mend, he ignores the advice and performs an expiatory sacrifice. He's apt to purify his house frequently, claiming that it is haunted by Hecate.[31] If owls hoot as he's walking along, he gets rattled and cries out "Mighty Athena!" before walking on. He refuses to step on a gravestone or view a corpse or visit a woman who's just given birth, claiming that it's in his interest to steer clear of impurity. Every fourth and seventh day of the month he orders his household

to boil down some wine.[32] He then goes out, buys myrtle, frankincense, and round cakes, and on returning home spends the whole day making wreaths for the Hermaphrodites.[33] Whenever he has a dream, he goes to the dream interpreters, to the seers, and to the augurs to ask which god or goddess he should supplicate. Every month he goes with his wife to be consecrated by the Orphic initiators[34] (or if she's too busy to accompany him, he goes with his children and their nurse). If he ever notices someone at the crossroads wreathed with garlic […], he goes away, bathes vigorously, summons priestesses, and tells them to purify him thoroughly with a sea onion or a dog.[35] If he catches sight of a madman or an epileptic, he shudders and spits into a fold of his cloak.[36]

"I wonder whether you're truly fond of me."

THE COMPLAINER

THE COMPLAINER IS THE SORT who, when his friend has sent him a portion from a sacrifice, says to the fellow delivering it, "He grudged me his broth and wine by not inviting me to the feast." When kissed by his mistress he says, "I wonder whether you're truly fond of me." He grumbles at Zeus not because it's raining, but because it didn't rain sooner. Finding a wallet on the street, he says, "Still, I've never found a treasure." On buying a slave for a fair price after driving a hard bargain, he says to the seller, "I wonder how healthy he could be, since I got him so cheap." To the man bringing the good news "You've had a son," he replies, "If you add, 'and half your estate is gone,' you'll be telling the truth." After winning a unanimous decision in a court case, he faults his speechwriter for having left out many sound arguments. When his friends have pooled their funds to lend him some money, and one of them says, "So cheer up!" he replies, "How can I? Haven't I got to pay each of you back and be grateful as well for the favor you've done me?"

He asks his wife whether she's locked the chest.

THE DISTRUSTFUL MAN

THE **D**ISTRUSTFUL MAN IS THE SORT who, when he's sent his slave to do some shopping, sends another along to find out how much the first one spent. Though he's carrying his money himself, he sits down every two hundred yards to count it. Lying down to sleep, he asks his wife whether she's locked the chest, and whether she's sealed the cupboard, and whether the courtyard has been bolted. And even if she says yes he gets out of bed anyway, naked and barefoot, lights a lamp, goes around looking into all these matters, and as a result barely gets a wink of sleep. When going to collect interest from people who owe him money, he takes witnesses along, so that his debtors can't deny the debt. He's apt to entrust his cloak not to the mender who does the best work, but to the one whose insurer is reliable. When someone comes to borrow drinking cups, he would prefer to refuse; but if it's a relative or someone he has to oblige, he hands them over only after weighing them and having their metals tested and all but getting someone to guarantee the cost of replacing them. He orders the slave who accompanies him to walk not behind but in front of him, so he can be sure the fellow doesn't run away. When people purchasing something from him say, "How much? Just put it on my tab. I haven't time at the moment," he replies, "Don't give it a thought; I'll just keep you company until you *do* have time."

He wipes his nose while eating and belches while drinking.

THE SLOVENLY MAN

THE SLOVENLY MAN IS THE SORT who, afflicted with dull-white eczema and black fingernails, goes about saying that these illnesses of his are hereditary. For *he* has them, as did his father and grandfather—so it's not easy to slip an illegitimate child into their family. He's also quite apt to have lesions on his shins and sores on his toes, and to let them fester rather than take care of them. His armpits are infested with lice and their hair hangs far down his sides. His teeth are black and rotting. He wipes his nose while eating, scratches himself while sacrificing, spits while talking, and belches while drinking. He lies down, unwashed, to sleep with his wife. Using rancid oil at the baths, he reeks of the pigsty. He goes out to the marketplace wearing a thick undergarment and a thin cloak covered with stains.

At dinner he relates that he's purged his gut from top to bottom.

THE VULGAR MAN

THE **V**ULGAR MAN IS THE SORT who goes in to awaken someone who's just gone to bed, to have a chat. He delays people who are about to set sail and asks visitors to wait while he takes his walk. Taking his baby from the nurse, he feeds it (after chewing its food himself), coos to it in baby talk, and calls it a worse rascal than its daddy.[37] At dinner he relates that by drinking hellebore he's purged his gut from top to bottom,[38] and that the bile in his excrement was blacker than the broth sitting on the table. He's apt, in front of his slaves, to say, "Tell me, mamma. When you were in labor and giving birth to me, what [...]?" He says he has a cold-water cistern at home, a garden with lots of fresh vegetables, and an excellent cook; that his house is an inn since it's always full; and that his friends are like a cracked wine jar: no matter how well he treats them, he can't fill them up. When entertaining, he points out to his dinner guests what an amazing fellow his lackey is. Over drinks he says that something's been arranged to amuse the company, and that they need only say the word and the slave will fetch her from the brothel-keeper, "so we can enjoy her... flute playing!"[39]

The sort who, when invited to dinner, is eager to sit next to the host.

The Social Climber

THE **S**OCIAL CLIMBER IS THE SORT who, when invited to dinner, is eager to sit next to his host. When it comes time for his son's hair to be cut, he takes the boy to Delphi and sees to it that the servant who attends him is an Ethiopian.[40] When paying back a mina of silver, he does so in coin newly minted. He's apt to buy a little ladder for the jackdaw that he's raised at home, and to make a tiny bronze shield for it to wear when it hops onto the ladder.[41] After sacrificing an ox,[42] he nails up the skull, turning its face toward the street and decking it with large wreaths so that his visitors see that he's sacrificed an ox. When he has paraded with the cavalry, he gives all his other gear to his slave to carry home, dons his cloak, and strolls around the marketplace in his spurs.[43] After his little Maltese dog has died, he builds a tomb and erects a small gravestone with the inscription "Melody of Malta." After dedicating a bronze finger in the shrine of Asclepius, he polishes, wreathes, and anoints it every day.[44] It's fair to assume that when his tribe is presiding, he gets his fellow councilors to assign *him* the task of bringing news of the sacrifice to the Assembly.[45] He then comes forward in a splendid cloak and wreath, and says, "Men of Athens, my colleagues and I have sacrificed the Galaxia to the Mother of the Gods, and the signs are favorable. Accept your good fortune."[46] After he's made this announcement, he goes home and tells his wife he's achieved a stunning success.

When a call for emergency funds is announced, she silently slips away.

THE PINCHPENNY

THE **P**INCHPENNY IS THE SORT who, when his tragic chorus wins first place, dedicates to Dionysus a strip of wood on which only his name has been written.[47] When a call for emergency funds is announced in the Assembly he gets up and silently slips away. When giving his daughter in marriage, he sells the meat from the sacrifices,[48] except for the priests' portion; the waiters hired for the wedding feast are told to bring their own food. When serving as ship's captain, he spreads the pilot's bedding on the deck for himself and stows away his own. He's apt not to send his children to school during the Muses' festival, but to say that they're ill, so they won't have to contribute anything. After shopping in the marketplace, he carries the vegetables home in the bosom of his robe.[49] He stays indoors whenever he's having his cloak washed.[50] If he learns that a friend is collecting contributions for a loan, he ducks out of the street when he sees the man approaching and takes the long way home. Though his wife brought him a dowry, he won't buy her a maid, but hires a slave from the women's market to accompany her on her outings. He wears shoes with soles that have been stitched back on and declares that they're as tough as horn. On rising in the morning, he tidies the house and rids the couches of bugs.[51] When taking a seat, he adjusts his threadbare cloak—the only thing he's wearing.[52]

He's apt to bamboozle a traveling companion.

THE CHARLATAN

CHARLATAN IS THE SORT who, standing in the bazaar at the Piraeus, tells foreigners that he has plenty of money invested in maritime concerns; he gives a detailed account of the money-lending business, and how much he's gained and lost; and while he's "shooting the long bow" about these matters, he sends his slave to the bank though he hasn't a single drachma in his account. He's apt to bamboozle a traveling companion by relating how he went on campaign with Alexander and got to know him, and how many gem-studded cups he brought home with him,[53] and declaring that the craftsmen in Asia are superior to those in Europe (asserting all this though he's never set foot out of the city). He says that he's received three letters from Antipater urging him to visit Macedonia,[54] and that though he's been granted the opportunity, duty-free, to export timber, he has refused it to avoid putting himself at the mercy of even one paid informer.[55] He claims that during the food shortage his expenditures on charitable gifts to the poor ran to more than five talents,[56] since he couldn't find it in his heart to refuse. When sitting next to people he doesn't know, he'll tell one of them to slide the abacus counters for him,

and then, calculating from the thousands column to the ones, and convincingly naming each beneficiary, he'll arrive at a total of ten talents and say that this figure represents the sums he has lent to friends—yet he hasn't included his subsidies for the fitting out of warships or all his other public benefactions. Going up to men selling thoroughbred horses, he pretends he wants to purchase one. Going to the clothing-sellers, he selects a wardrobe that costs two talents, and then scolds his slave for not having brought along the money. Though he's living in a rented house, he tells someone who's not in the know that the house was inherited from his father and that he's planning to sell it since it's too small for entertaining.

He won't speak to passersby, looking up only when it suits him.

THE ARROGANT MAN

THE **A**RROGANT MAN IS THE SORT who says to someone who's pressed for time that he'll meet him after dinner while taking his walk. He says he never forgets that he's done someone a favor. Engaged as an arbitrator, he presents his decision to the disputants while walking down the street. When appointed to office he declares under oath that he cannot serve, as he has no time. He won't approach another man first. He's apt to tell those who are selling something or seeking employment to come to him first thing in the morning. When walking down the street, he won't speak to passersby, but keeps his head lowered, looking up only when it suits him. When entertaining friends, he doesn't dine with them, but orders one of his subordinates to see to their needs. Whenever he's going somewhere, he sends someone on ahead to say that he's on his way. He admits no one into his presence when he's anointing himself, bathing, or eating. When settling an account with someone, he's sure to have his slave slide the counters, compute the total, and write out an invoice.[57] When sending a message, he doesn't write "You would be doing me a favor," but rather "I wish this done" and "I've sent someone to you to pick it up" and "Nothing else will do" and "Be quick about it."

He does anything but fight the enemy.

The Coward

THE **C**OWARD IS THE SORT who, when he's at sea, declares that the headlands are pirate ships. When there's a big swell, he asks whether anyone on board has not been initiated into the Mysteries.[58] Glancing skyward, he asks the helmsman whether they're halfway there and how the weather strikes him; he tells the man sitting next to him that he's afraid because of a dream. Stripping off his tunic, he gives it to his slave and begs to be put ashore. When he's serving in the military and the infantry are advancing to attack, he calls to his comrades and urges them to stand alongside him first and survey the field, saying it's hard to tell which men are the enemy. Hearing a roar and seeing men falling, he tells his comrades that in his haste he forgot to bring his sword. He then runs to his tent and sends his slave outside, ordering him to see where the enemy troops are. Hiding the sword under his pillow, he then spends a long time pretending to search for it. When from within the tent he sees one of his friends being brought back wounded, he runs up to him, urges him to be brave, and helps carry him inside. He then attends to him carefully, sponges him, sits beside him, whisks the flies away from his wound, and does anything but fight the enemy. When the trumpeter

sounds the charge, he sits in the tent, saying, "Hang the man! He won't let a fellow get any sleep with his incessant signaling." Drenched with blood from the other man's wound, he meets the men returning from battle and reports (as if he'd been in some danger), "I saved one of our friends." He then brings the members of his tribe inside to see the wounded man and tells each of them that he carried the man into the tent with his own hands.

He struts about making theatrical pronouncements.

THE AUTHORITARIAN

THE AUTHORITARIAN IS THE SORT who, when the people are deliberating about whom they'll choose to help the chief magistrate organize the procession, comes forward and declares that the assistants should be granted absolute power.[59] If someone proposes that there be ten, he says, "One is sufficient, though he should be a real man." The only verse of Homer that he recalls is, "Mob rule is no good thing; let there be one ruler";[60] of the other verses he is ignorant. He's quite apt to make remarks like, "We must form a league and deliberate about these matters, and get free of the mob and the marketplace, and we should stop running for office and thereby cease depending on their insults or their honors," and "Either *they* have to live in this city, or *we* do." He goes out at noon, sporting his cloak, his hair cut to a medium length, and his finger-nails carefully trimmed, and struts about making theatrical pronouncements: "The paid informers are making the city unlivable,"[61] "We're badly hurt by corruption in the courts," "I wonder what people who pursue public careers really want," and "The common people are ungrateful, though they receive plenty of handouts and gifts." He says he's ashamed in the Assembly when some scrawny, unwashed fellow sits next to him. He says, "Aren't we being ruined by public duties and the obligation to fit out warships?"[62] and "The demagogues are an odious breed," declaring that Theseus was responsible, in the first place, for the city's troubles, since in the course of combining twelve cities into one [...] But he got what he deserved, since he was the first man they killed.[63]

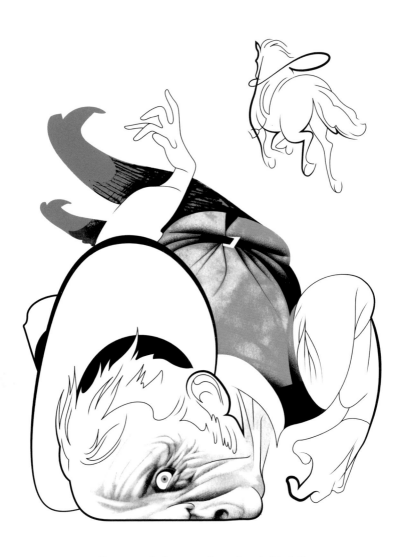

He practices his horsemanship and cracks his skull.

THE LATE LEARNER

THE **L**ATE LEARNER IS THE SORT who at sixty commits speeches to memory, but when reciting them at a drinking party forgets the words. From his son he learns "right face," "left face," and "about face."[64] At the hero-festivals he joins the boys in the torch race. If he's invited to a temple of Heracles, he's sure to throw off his cloak and try to lift the bull in order to put a neck lock on it.[65] He frequents the wrestling schools and challenges the athletes. He sits through theatrical shows three or four times, trying to learn the songs. When he's being initiated in the rites of Sabazius, he's eager for the priest to think *him* the handsomest initiate.[66] Smitten with a prostitute, he assaults her door with a battering ram, gets beaten up by her other lover, and then sues the fellow. Riding into the country on a borrowed horse, he practices his horsemanship, takes a header, and cracks his skull. He competes in archery and the javelin with the instructor of his sons and urges them to take some pointers from himself, since their instructor is incompetent. Practicing his wrestling at the baths, he frequently swivels his hips so as to appear proficient. When women are nearby, he practices his dance steps while humming to himself.

She's sure to join in when others are speaking ill of anyone.

THE SLANDERER

THE **S**LANDERER IS THE SORT who, when asked, "Who is so-and-so?" replies in the manner of a genealogist, saying, "I'll begin with his ancestors. The man's father was originally named Sosias, but in the army became Sosistratus, and when enrolled as a townsman, Sosidemus.[67] His mother, however, is a wellborn Thracian. Her name, at any rate, is [...]; and such women, in *her* country, are said to be wellborn. So this man, as one might expect with such parents, is a rascal with a tattoo."[68] He says, "These women snatch passersby from the street," and "The legs in this house are up in the air. Indeed the old saying, 'They copulate in the street like bitches,' is no joke" and "In short, they are vixens," and "They answer their front doors themselves."[69] He's sure to join in when others are speaking ill of anyone, saying, "I've come to hate that man more than anyone. His face is hideous, his villainy unequaled. And here's a proof: his wife brought him a dowry of a talent; yet from the day she bore him a son he's given her three coppers a day for groceries and makes her bathe in cold water throughout the month of Poseideon."[70] When sitting in company, he's apt to talk about someone who's just left; and once started, he doesn't stop until he's maligned the man's relatives. He's especially given to speaking ill of his own friends and relatives (including the dead), declares that slander is just another word for free speech, democracy, and liberty, and gets more pleasure from it than from anything else in his life.

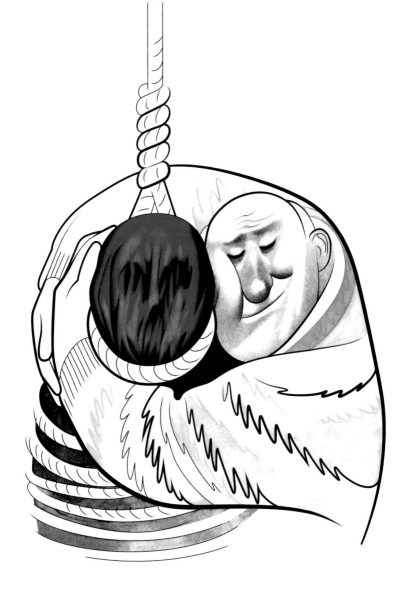

He's apt to champion villains and to testify on their behalf.

THE FRIEND OF SCOUNDRELS

THE FRIEND OF SCOUNDRELS IS THE SORT who fraternizes with men who have been defeated in court and convicted in public trials; he assumes that if he's friendly with them, he'll become more worldly and formidable. In speaking of men who are good, he says that [...] and claims that no one is good and that everyone's the same, and he will mockingly remark, "How worthy he is!" He calls the rogue "an independent thinker," and though he agrees that some of the things said about the man are true, [...] he says that the man is good-natured, congenial, and clever, and earnestly maintains that he himself has never met a more capable fellow. He's well disposed when the man speaks in the Assembly or defends himself in court, and he's apt to tell the jurors, "One must judge the case, not the man." He maintains that the man is the people's watchdog (since he barks at those who injure them) and says, "We won't have anyone willing to take trouble on behalf of the public good if we reject such men." He's apt to champion villains and to testify on their behalf and when serving on a jury to disparage the arguments presented by both parties.

When distributing portions, he hastens to give himself a double share.

THE CHISELER

THE **C**HISELER IS THE SORT who, when giving a banquet, doesn't serve enough bread. He borrows money from a foreigner who's staying at his house.[71] When distributing portions, he says it's fair for the distributor to receive a double share and hastens to give himself one. If he's selling wine, he sells his friend a batch that's been watered down. He goes to the theater with his sons only when the managers aren't charging admission. When going abroad on public business, he leaves his traveling stipend at home and borrows from his fellow envoys. He loads his attendant with more baggage than he can carry and supplies him with fewer provisions than anyone else. He demands his share of any presents they receive and then sells them. Anointing himself at the baths, he says to his slave, "The oil you bought is rancid," and uses someone else's. When his slaves find coins in the street, he's apt to demand a share, saying, "Hermes does not play favorites." When he's sent his cloak out to be cleaned, he borrows one from an acquaintance and trails around in it for several days until he's asked to return it. After hammering the base of a Pheidonian measuring cup upwards,[72] he personally measures out provisions for his domestic servants, taking care that the cup's contents lie

precisely level with the brim. He can be counted on, when repaying a debt of thirty minas, to return an amount that falls short by four drachmas.[73] If his sons miss school because of illness, he deducts a proportional amount from their tuition, and he won't send them to their lessons for the entire month of Anthesterion, since there are so many spectacles, to avoid the expense. When collecting rent from a slave, he includes a charge for the cost of exchanging the copper.[74] When hosting a dinner for his clan, he asks that his slaves' food be paid for out of the common fund, though he submits an account of the radish-halves left after the meal so that the slaves waiting at table won't take them. When abroad with acquaintances, he uses their slaves, hires out his own, and doesn't deposit the proceeds in their common fund. When people meet for a meal at his house, he's sure to charge the company for firewood, lentils, vinegar, salt, and the lamp oil he's supplied. If one of his friends is getting married or giving his daughter in marriage, he leaves town ahead of time to avoid having to send a present. He borrows from acquaintances the sorts of things one wouldn't demand back, or wouldn't retrieve should people offer to return them.

Annotations

The Dissembler

1. The Greek is *eirôn*, root of the English "irony," an untranslatable and complex word that implies a pretense of ignorance, deception, and a kind of superiority attained by concealment. In Plato's dialogues, Socrates is often called an *eirôn* by interlocutors who sense he is asking questions in a naïve way when he in fact knows the answers already.

2. Athenians were extremely litigious, so losing a lawsuit would be a common sort of setback.

The Flatterer

3. The Flatterer's companion goes unnamed and uncharacterized, but presumably is the same man throughout, since a flatterer (*kolax* in Greek) would normally attach himself to a single "host"—a wealthy individual from whom he might expect money or meals.

4. There were three stoas, or public porticos, in the Athenian market square; the Stoa Poikile (or Painted Stoa) in particular was a favored place for leisurely conversations. It became a kind of informal lecture hall for students of Zeno of Citium, who thus became known as the Stoics.

5. The Greeks apparently used the expression "plucking at threads" to connote servile adulation.

The Talker

6. The Greater or City Dionysia was a festival occurring in March, roughly the season in which moderating Aegean weather permitted seafaring to resume after a winter hiatus. No doubt the resumption of sailing explains the affordability of wheat mentioned earlier by the Talker, since Athens imported much of its grain by ship.

7. The rites of the Mysteries at Eleusis, a cult devoted to the worship of Demeter and Persephone, involved a torchlight procession.

8. The three religious festivals mentioned were widely known to Athenians, so no reminders of their dates would be needed. The Rustic Dionysia took place at a different time than the City Dionysia mentioned above.

The Yokel

9. Sessions of the *Ekklesia*, the open-air meetings that all Athenian citizens could attend to cast their votes, were occasions that might bring rustics like the Yokel into the city from the surrounding countryside.

10. Thus indecorously exposing his private parts.

11. Greeks normally mixed wine with water in varying proportions that diluted the wine by more than half. To drink it "neat" was a barbarian custom.

12. As opposed to having his slave do it.

13. Sandals with protruding nails, like the modern "hobnailed boot," were designed for toughness and durability.

14. Since both were cheap commodities, he broadcasts his hope for a bargain.

15. Market fairs in ancient Athens were often held on the first day of the lunar month.

The Sycophant

16. It has been suggested that these shouts accompany hand gestures, as in the modern "Rock, Paper, Scissors."

The Senseless Man

17. An obscene and silly dance, thought appropriate only for drunkards.

18. A usurious daily rate of 25 percent.

19. Storing money in the mouth was a common practice among Greeks, whose clothing lacked pockets.

The Babbler

20. The verbal showdown that took place "in the time of Aristophon" might be the famous debate at Athens between Aeschines and Demosthenes in 330 BC, a year in which a man named Aristophon held the office of archon (though there were two other Aristophons who lived slightly earlier). Lysander, the admiral who helped win the Peloponnesian War for Sparta, must have taken part in many debates at Sparta (i.e., "among the Lacedemonians") in the late fifth and early fourth centuries BC.

21. The Babbler may well have been among the 9,000 wealthiest citizens who, as of 321 BC (around the time that *Characters* was likely composed), were alone accorded the right to speak and vote in the Assembly. That would explain why he looks down on "the masses," who had recently been stripped of that right.

The Newshound

22. Cassander, who controlled Macedonia and parts of Greece in the years following 319 BC, was engaged at various times in a power struggle with Polyperchon, one of Alexander the Great's former generals, but was never defeated or taken prisoner—making the Newshound a monger not only of rumors, but of false ones.

The Miser

23. A tiny sum.

24. Greek land lots were marked out by boundary stones, which could be easily moved.

25. The last three items were used in ritual sacrifices; the "wreaths" were fillets of wool wrapped around the horns of the sacrificial animal.

The Obnoxious Man

26. The point seems to be that passersby would never feel entitled to partake in such an intimate evening. The flute girls were only nominally musicians; they were also expected to provide sexual favors.

The Busybody

27. More information than is found on surviving Attic tombstones, which (in the case of Athenian citizens at least) did not often list the mother of the deceased and never eulogized family members.

The Superstitious Man

28. The first two actions would be appropriate before a religious rite, not for every day. Laurel was used as a protective charm, much like garlic in some cultures today.

29. Sabazius was a foreign deity sometimes identified by the Greeks with Dionysus; snake handling was a feature of his cult. "Holy" was a variety of poisonous snake, here taken to be an incarnation of a "hero" or semidivine being.

30. A ritual to obtain good fortune.

31. A goddess of the underworld.

32. The fourth and seventh days were sacred to Hermes and Apollo, respectively; the wine reduction was presumably intended for ritual use.

33. Hermaphroditus, the child of Hermes and Aphrodite, was worshipped as a personal protector in the household of the Suspicious Man, who wreathes the god's many statues with garlands at times of stress.

34. These *Orpheotelestai* were wandering priests who specialized in purifications.

35. These creatures would have been carried around the Suspicious Man in a circle as a purificatory rite.

36. Spitting, either into one's hands or inside one's clothes, is still practiced today in some cultures as a way to avoid evil omens.

The Vulgar Man

37. All behavior properly left to the nurse.

38. A plant extract commonly used as a medical purgative or emetic.

39. Flute girls at Greek drinking parties are often depicted as freely available sexual partners, but it was unusual (and perhaps low-class) to summon one from a brothel.

THE SOCIAL CLIMBER

40. Ethiopian slaves were rare in the Greek world at this time and therefore fashionable. Adolescents in Greece would traditionally cut their hair as a rite of passage into adulthood, and mythic heroes sometimes dedicated the cut locks in Apollo's shrine at Delphi; for an ordinary citizen to do this would be extravagant.

41. The bird thus imitates a Greek soldier scaling a wall in a siege.

42. An expensive sacrificial animal, beyond the means of most people.

43 Thus showing that he belongs to the *hippeis*, the class of citizens wealthy enough to own horses.

44. Effigies of body parts were routinely dedicated to Asclepius, the god of healing, by people afflicted in those parts. Here the Social Climber engages in an extravagant ritual over a presumably minor injury.

45. Athenian citizens took turns serving on the *Boulê*, an executive board supervising the larger Assembly, and leadership of the *Boulê* rotated among its members "according to their tribe." So even an ordinary citizen might get the chance, once or twice in his life, to occupy this high office. The Social Climber here tries to make the most of his big moment, though his responsibility is comically small.

46. A bit of rhetorical pomposity for a routine ritual offering of a bowl of Galaxia, a kind of barley porridge.

THE PINCHPENNY

47. Wealthy Athenians undertook to sponsor the tragic performances that took place every year at the festival of Dionysus as part of a competition among three chosen playwrights. It was a great honor for the sponsor if his production won, and a substantial offering to Dionysus usually followed.

48. Normally it would be offered to the guests.

49. So as not to pay an attendant to do so.

50. Rather than spring for a spare.

51. That is, he cleans it himself rather than buying a slave.

52. To wear a *tribón*, a rough, coarse cloak, with no soft tunic underneath was a mark of ascetic practice, appropriate for rugged Spartans. Here the Pinchpenny seems to avoid sitting on the cloak to make it last longer.

The Charlatan
53. Alexander the Great's campaign through Asia (334–323 BC) had made many common soldiers vastly rich.

54. Antipater served as the top Macedonian officer in Europe while Alexander was alive and became a kind of regent there following Alexander's death.

55. Macedonia and Athens were briefly at war in the year after Alexander's death, and presumably the Charlatan fears an indictment for trading with an enemy nation.

56. A vast sum, each talent worth 6,000 drachmas. The two talents that the Charlatan plans to spend on clothing would be enough to buy stacks of the most precious garments.

The Arrogant Man
57. That is, he assigns to his slave a sensitive task that one would normally perform oneself.

The Coward
58. Initiation into various Greek mystery cults was thought to confer the special protection of the gods; the Coward here inverts the idea and considers a non-initiate a threat.

59. The Greek term is *oligarchikos*, "the oligarchic man"—that is, one who favors a government by the few. The oligarchic faction at Athens succeeded on several occasions in seizing control of the government and stripping out key provisions of the democratic constitution. The procession in question took place at the City Dionysia, an annual festival in Athens; it was organized by a board of ten, but to grant these men "absolute power," as the authoritarian suggests, would be bizarrely out of proportion with their small roles.

60. The quote is from the *Iliad* (2.204), where Odysseus speaks in support of Agamemnon.

61. Sycophants, who received financial rewards for bringing indictments. The Authoritarian hates this profession because it falls largely to the poor, as did other juridical offices and minor magistracies.

62. The obligation to sponsor triremes, Greek military vessels crewed by 170 rowers, was one of several public benefactions that fell to the Athenian rich.

63. In myth, Theseus was the Athenian king who united disparate villages to create the city of Athens. He was ousted by a rebel leader named Menestheus, sometimes characterized in Greek lore as a demagogue, and was slain by the king with whom he sought refuge.

THE LATE LEARNER

64. Commands of military drill, perhaps of a kind introduced after the Late Learner's years of service.

65. At Greek religious rites, teams of youths would lift the sacrificial bull as a demonstration of strength, with some pulling back the head to bare its neck to the slaughterer's knife.

66. Initiations into mystery cults were occasions for dressing up and looking one's best. Sabazius was a foreign deity imported into Greece in the classical era.

The Slanderer

67. "Army" in Greek is *stratos* and "town" is *demos*, so this man's father appears to change his name to fit whatever place he lands in. His original name, Sosias, typically used for slaves in theater comedies, may imply that he once was one himself.

68. Tattooing was a Thracian custom, and the mother's name, missing from the manuscripts, presumably alluded to tattoos. A Thracian (i.e., non-Greek) mother would disqualify the Slanderer's victim from Athenian citizenship.

69. All four slanders are spoken as though the Slanderer were pointing to a house he takes to be a brothel. Respectable women would have their slaves answer the door.

70. Poseideon is a winter month generally corresponding to our December/January.

The Chiseler

71. The foreigner would have a hard time bringing legal action if the Chiseler failed to repay.

72. The Pheidonian measure was less full than the standard one used in Athens at this time, and the ration would be further reduced by a hammered-in bottom.

73. That is, four drachmas short of three thousand. The Athenians used a large coin worth four drachmas, so the Chiseler meanly omits a single coin.

74. Slaves who were allowed to run their own businesses were obliged to give their masters a percentage of the proceeds, paid here in copper coin that the Chiseler converts to silver.

Acknowledgments

The editor and translator wish to thank our
illustrator, André Carrilho; designer, Don Quaintance;
text editor, Prudence Crowther; and publishers
Manuela Roosevelt and Nicholas Callaway.

CONTRIBUTORS

JAMES ROMM is an author, reviewer, and the James H. Ottaway Jr. Professor of Classics at Bard College in Annandale, New York. His reviews and essays have appeared in the *London Review of Books* and *The New York Times Book Review*, among other publications. His books include *Ghost on the Throne: The Death of Alexander the Great and the War for Crown and Empire* (Knopf, 2011) and *Dying Every Day: Seneca at the Court of Nero* (Knopf, 2014). He and Pamela Mensch have collaborated on annotated translations of numerous Greek authors.

PAMELA MENSCH is a translator of ancient Greek literature who lives in New York City. Her translations include *The Landmark Arrian: The Campaigns of Alexander* (Pantheon, 2012), *Histories: Herodotus* (Hackett, 2014), *The Age of Caesar: Five Roman Lives, Plutarch* (Norton, 2017), and *Lives of the Eminent Philosophers: Diogenes Laertius* (Oxford, 2018).

ANDRÉ CARRILHO is a designer, illustrator, caricaturist, and animator from Lisbon. He has shown his work in group and solo exhibitions in Brazil, China, France, Portugal, Spain, and the United States. His drawings have been published by *Diário de Notícias*, *Harper's*, *New York Magazine*, *The New York Times*, *The New Yorker*, *NZZ am Sonntag*, and *Vanity Fair*, among other newspapers and magazines.

DON QUAINTANCE is a graphic designer who lives in Houston. He has designed over one hundred and fifty art-related monographs including *Leonardo's Incessant Last Supper*, *Marcel Duchamp: Étant donnés* (George Wittenborn Award), and recent museum retrospectives for Alberto Burri, John Chamberlain, Max Ernst, Arshile Gorky, Barnett Newman, Robert Rauschenberg, and James Rosenquist.

Published by
CALLAWAY ARTS & ENTERTAINMENT
41 Union Square, Suite 1101
New York, New York 10003
www.callaway.com

ISBN 978-0-935112-37-5

First Edition
Printed in Germany

Distributed in the U.S. by Ingram Publisher Services
www.ingramcontent.com

Library of Congress Cataloguing-in-Publication Data

Names: Theophrastus author. | Romm, James S. author of introduction. |
  Mensch, Pamela, 1956- translator. | Carrilho, André illustrator.
Title: Characters : an ancient take on bad behavior / Theophrastus ;
  introduction and annotations James Romm ; translation, Pamela Mensch ;
  illustrations, André Carrilho ; graphic design, Don Quaintance.
Other titles: Characters. English
Description: New York : Callaway, 2018. Identifiers: LCCN 2018000607 | ISBN
9780935112375 (hardcover : alk. paper)
Subjects: LCSH: Character sketches.
Classification: LCC PA4449.E5 C5 2018 | DDC 888/.01--dc23
LC record available at https://lccn.loc.gov/2018000607